The Little
Chagall

Catherine de Duve

A journey to the country of the Russian painter

KATE'ART
EDITIONS

MARC CHAGALL'S

Chagall liked to paint pictures of Russia, the country where he was born. He painted the countryside, villages, peasants, cows being milked, farm animals: horses, pigs, goats, cats, cockerels etc. His paintings were poetic, and he let his imagination take flight…

Folklore

Moon

Farm animals

Human animals

Circus

Upside-down houses

Violinist

Branches in flower

Lovers

RUSSIA

At the time of Chagall, Russia was governed by its last emperor, Tsar Nicholas II. But in 1917 the Revolution, led by Lenin (1870 – 1924), brought the rule of the Tsars to an end. The Bolsheviks (or Soviets) – a political party representing workers - came to power. The capital, Saint Petersburg, was given a new name: Leningrad. This (1922) was the start of the Soviet Union, which would not become Russia again until 1991.

The Revolution

MARC CHAGALL

Fire, fire! Flames were sweeping through the poor Jewish district of Vitebsk, in Belarus. In one of these small wooden houses, Movcha (Moses) – Marc Chagall – had just been born. It was July 7th, 1887. The baby was saved from the fire!

Marc was the eldest of nine children. He was so shy that he stammered when he talked. His life revolved around visits to the synagogue, religious festivals, work on the land and his house in the "shtetl", the Jewish quarter. His parents, Zakhar and Feïga-Ita, were *illiterate*. His father worked in a herring warehouse and his mother ran the family grocery shop. Marc often spent his holidays with his grandfather, a butcher and ritual slaughterer. He watched in terror as the animals he loved so much – cows, donkeys, cockerels and horses – were put to death. Their memory would stay with him.

Illiterate: *someone who can not read or write*

Can you find an animal-trader, a billy-goat and a foal? Where are they heading for in the darkness?

Marc's mum enrolled her son in the Russian school where he met children from outside the "shtetl", which was all he had known up to then. At school, Marc was a dreamer, and from the age of 13, he was passionate about drawing. His best friend was Ossip Zadkine, who would also become an artist. After school, Chagall decided to be a painter. He worked in an artist's studio, then went to Saint Petersburg to art school. He also took violin and singing lessons. Marc Chagall dreamt of becoming a great artist!

In 1909 he met Bella Rosenfeld, a jeweller's daughter. They fell madly in love, but Chagall was keen to travel! Bye bye Russia!

A soldier in the green uniform of the Russian special brigade, serving under the Imperial Government, points at the *samovar*. What is in it? His eyes are different colours. His cap seems to have leapt up from his bald head. He has a wonderful moustache! A pair of dolls appear to be dancing on the table. What can we see through the window? A typical Russian house, an *isba*.

Chagall applied his paint in the same way as the cubist or futurist painters, with different facets and geometrical shapes. He sometimes used modern painting techniques, but still had his own special style.

A samovar *is a sort of large Russian kettle.*
An isba *is a traditional wooden Russian house, rather like a chalet.*

Find the cubist and futurist-style "facets". And look at the details in these circles. Can you find them in the picture?

To find out more about Cubism see *The Little Picasso* in the same collection: pp. 12-19.

LA RUCHE

Off to Paris! In May 1911, after a four-day train journey, Chagall arrived in Paris, the art capital of the world, where Russian artists were then fashionable. Marc found his first studio in Montmartre and settled there. He could only speak Russian and Yiddish. He missed his country…but Paris was bursting with creativity, and Chagall visited the museums and exhibitions. He marvelled at the paintings of Manet, Courbet and Delacroix, and loved the colours used by Van Gogh, Gauguin and Matisse*.

Chagall moved into one of the 140 rather run-down studios in La Ruche ("The Beehive"), a wooden building housing a community of artists, poets, painters and sculptors from all over the world, such as Léger, Modigliani, Soutine, Zadkine, etc. He was so far from home that his thoughts turned lovingly to Russia. For his art he chose subjects from Jewish folklore and life in the "shtetl", and used memories from his childhood in this picture, *I and the Village*.

Look at the picture. Who or what is upside-down?
Use each detail to tell a story, and work out the order
of events. Once upon a time in a village...

* To find out more about these artists, see *The Little Manet*, *The Little Matisse*, *The Little Van Gogh* and *The Little Gauguin* in the same series.

SELF-PORTRAIT

The painter is working, facing his easel. The colours are jostling one another on his palette. Once again, he is painting scenes from his beloved Russia. A synagogue floats in a small cloud, a memory that sticks in his mind. But what can we see through the window? It's the Eiffel Tower! On the walls of the studio are the Yiddish words for "Russia" and "Paris". Which picture is Chagall painting here?

 Find the man with the parachute. How many fingers does the painter have? Do you know why he has so many?

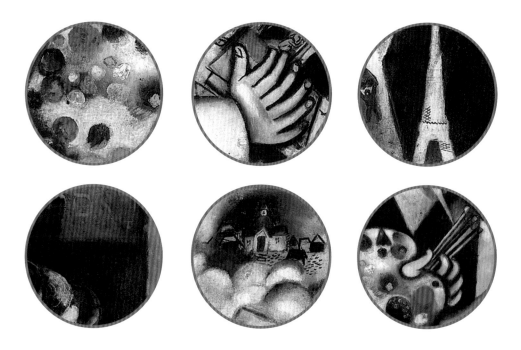

In Yiddish, working "with all seven fingers" means to do your utmost, to use all your skills and talents.

BELLA

B ella had been waiting for him for four years! Chagall returned to Russia and was reunited with her. He was glad to be back with his muse. He painted their happiness together, and, since the First World War (1914 – 1918) had been declared, was unable to return to Paris. Bella and Chagall were married on the 25th of July 1915. Their daughter Ida was born one year later.

How old was Chagall in 1915, when he painted the picture opposite? Find the details below in the picture.

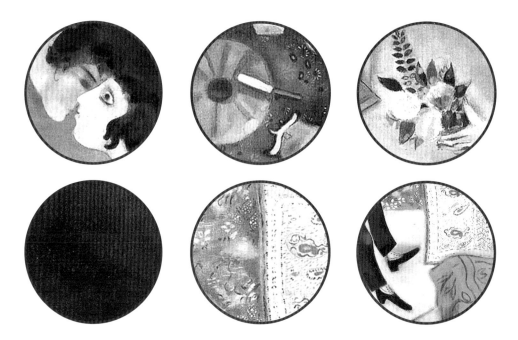

Happy Birthday!

Chagall was now a recognised artist. He had already had his first individual exhibition in Berlin. In the countryside he painted this picture, *The Birthday*. The couple are flying in their home on the wings of love, and kiss tenderly. A bunch of flowers symbolises their joy, and the love they share. The red floor is like a bright red heart. On the table, covered with a blue flowered tablecloth, a birthday cake is about to be cut. Happy Birthday!

'CHAGALL'S BOX'

In 1917 Russia was in the middle of a revolution. Chagall was appointed Commissioner for Fine Arts in Vitebsk, the town where he was born. Together with other artists, he set up an academy, with 900 pupils. He wanted to bring art to the people. The town was decorated with large flags showing painted animals. The authorities thought it was all too fanciful, and in 1920 he was replaced by Malevich, a professor and painter. Fortunately, Chagall then received an unexpected offer of work. The Jewish theatre in Moscow commissioned him to paint nine huge decorative panels. On them he painted his favourite ideas and images. He was 33 years old and at the height of his artistic abilities.

Dance *Music* *Theatre*

Chagall was fascinated by the world of the theatre, and made the sets, costumes, ceiling and curtains. His imaginative style was everywhere! The little theatre would be known as "Chagall's Box".

See if you can create your own "box" in the space below, to decorate your bedroom from the ceiling to the curtains!

CHAGALL THE POET

In 1923, disappointed by how little freedom artists had in Russia, Chagall left the country. Fortunately he received support from admirers and friends, including the poet Blaise Cendrars and the famous art dealer Ambroise Vollard. Chagall loved the world of literature. He preferred the company of writers and poets such as Aragon and Eluard, or Apollinaire, who described Chagall's art as "supernatural".

Chagall himself turned his hand to poetry, and wrote a collection of poems between 1930 and 1935.

At night, an angel flies in the sky
A white flash over the rooftops
He speaks to me of a long, long path ahead
He will cry out my name above the houses

Extract from "My Distant Home", *Poems*

Can you illustrate this poem by Chagall?

THE FIDDLER

The violin-player has a green head and a long coat - half white, half checked. His feet are dangling, floating in the air, as he plays music and dances. Where are we? In a Russian village covered in snow. Can you see any footprints? A bush is already flowering, and birds are pecking for food. How many can you spot?

Chagall arranges the figures in his paintings in the same way as in the religious scenes of the Middle Ages, according to how important they are to him. He follows his heart, not the rules of logic.

Look at the way the picture is composed. List the various elements in the picture, starting with the most prominent, and ending with those in the background.

Ten years later, Chagall painted another violinist, this time wearing a purple coat, the colour of mysticism. Was he remembering his uncle Neuch, who used to play the violin each *Sabbath* day? Here he is dancing on the rooftops. Chagall painted violins all his life, sometimes next to a cow, sometimes being played by the moon…

The sabbath is the day of rest, the seventh day of the Jewish week. It lasts from Friday before sunset until Saturday after the stars come out.

Compare the two violinists painted by Chagall. Which do you like best?

In 1924, Chagall held his first *retrospective*, and two years later had his first exhibition in New York.

A retrospective is an exhibition which looks back over an artist's career, and shows early works as well as more recent ones.

THE EIFFEL TOWER

In 1923 Chagall emigrated to Paris. He was now more confident and no longer stammered. "I needed Paris as a tree needs water", he wrote. He also said that he liked its "blueness". In Paris, Chagall felt free and happy. His art tells stories rather like fairy tales. Look! There's the Eiffel Tower riding a donkey and smoking a pipe! Why is the donkey all dressed up? Night changes everything. Two moons meet above the sleeping city. Animals put on clothes and become human. Chagall painted his dream using gouache on card.

 Draw one of your dreams.

We're in the middle of the countryside, surrounded by cows and donkeys. We feel very much at home with them...)

"My Life", Chagall

Chagall and his family travelled all around France. Marc was happy. In the countryside he was back amongst the country-people and animals of his childhood.

Chagall then suggested to Vollard a very "French" project. He wanted to illustrate the famous fables of the French poet La Fontaine (1621-1695). Do you know any of these? The pictures show Chagall's great love of animals.

He created a fantasy world and ignored the moral aspect of the fables. He began a series of lively gouache drawings.

The cockerel and the fox

The Fox and the grapes
Calvet-Rogniat
(1813-1875)

The Fox and the Grapes

A fox, almost with hunger dying,
Some grapes upon a trellis spying,
To all appearance ripe, clad in
Their tempting russet skin,
Most gladly would have eat them;
But since he could not get them,
So far above 'his reach the vine--
'They're sour,' he said; 'such grapes as these,
The dogs may eat them if they please!'
Did he not better than to whine?

LA FONTAINE

 Choose one of the fables of La Fontaine and illustrate it.

THE CIRCUS

> For me, the circus is a magical show, which is here and then gone – a whole new world.

Marc Chagall loved circuses! He filled his pictures with acrobats, jugglers, clowns, dancers, musicians and magicians. He would go to the Cirque d'Hiver, the Winter Circus, where Vollard, the art dealer, would invite artists to join him in his box, to gain inspiration from the magical world of the circus. This is Chagall's first circus picture. The composition is balanced and well-structured. Could he have been influenced by a certain Pablo Picasso?

What would you rather be? An acrobat, bareback rider, clown, trapeze artist or lion-tamer? Draw your act in the show.

THE BIBLE

Chagall read the Bible regularly from when he was a little child. It fed his spirit and he used it as a source of poetry. In 1931 he travelled to Palestine, where he visited the Jewish holy places. In Poland he became aware of the dark times in which he was living. Chagall would no longer choose images from folklore for his paintings, but instead he began to show the suffering of his people.

The Torah is made up of five books containing God's teachings handed down through Moses.

Chagall took French nationality in 1937. Then the Second World War (1939 – 1945) broke out. Jews were increasingly persecuted: there were arrests, raids, deportations etc. Chagall and his family left for America and reached New York on the 23rd of June 1941, the same day as the Germans attacked the USSR, formerly Russia, their homeland.

Chagall received a warm welcome, although he spoke no English. But in 1944, Bella suddenly fell ill, and died a few days later. "Everything has become dark to my eyes", said Chagall, who was devastated by his loss.

Find Christ on the Cross in the painting and match up these details: the Rabbi, the Cow, the Torah, the Wandering Jew and the Synagogue in flames.

In 1948, Marc Chagall returned to France. In 1950, he settled in the South, at Saint-Jean-Cap-Ferrat. Two years later, at the age of 65, Marc married Valentina Brodsky, known as Vava. She was also of Russian origin. He had found happiness once again! He travelled to Russia in 1973, after more then fifty years away.

Chagall dreamt of a world where nations would be united in love. His art was again full of hope. He was commissioned to create stained glass windows for churches and synagogues. He loved the interplay of light and colours and worked hard with the master glassworkers.

Design and colour these windows in colours which will
let through the light. Create a magical atmosphere.

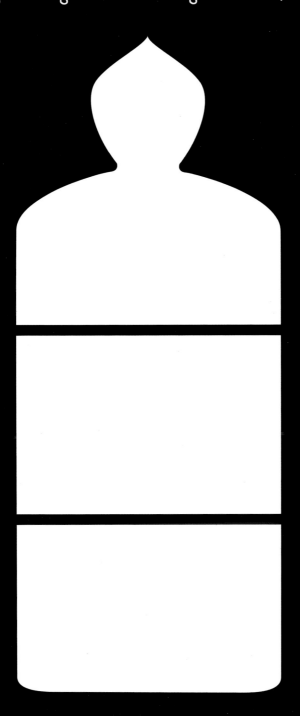

THE OPERA

Chagall came back from America with new approaches to painting, inspired by the monumental art he had seen. In 1963, Andre Malraux, the Minister of Culture, commissioned him to decorate the ceiling of the Paris Opera. Chagall divided his composition into five sections of different colours, dedicating each to the famous works of different composers.
Can you see Berlioz and Wagner's masterpieces in green, Tchaikovsky's in yellow, Mozart and Mussorgsky's in blue, Ravel and Stravinsky's in red and Debussy and Rameau's in white?

Look at the beautiful ceiling of the Opera. Can you find the swan from Tchaikovsky's ballet "Swan Lake" and Papageno from Mozart's "The Magic Flute"?

In 1967, Chagall had a house built in Saint-Paul-de-Vence, in the South of France. In 1973 he helped inaugurate the Chagall Museum, *the Musée National Message Biblique Marc Chagall*, in Nice. Marc Chagall passed away on the 28th of March 1985, at the age of 97.

Text: Catherine de Duve
Concept and Production: Kate'Art Editions
Contributors: Aurore t' Kint, Véronique Lux, Carole Daprey
Translation from the French: Rachel Beasley

AMSTERDAM, Stedelijk Museum: *Self-Portrait with Seven Digits*, 1912-1913: p. 10 (details), p. 11 ; *The Fiddler*, 1912-1913: cover (detail), p. 2 (detail), p. 18 |BASEL, Öffentliche Kunstsammlung - Kunstmuseum: *The Cattle Dealer*, 1912 : p. 4 |BRUSSELS, The Royal Museums of Fine-Arts of Belgium: *The Eiffel Tower. The Dream. Eiffel Tower and the Donkey*, 1927: p. 2 (detail), p. 21 | CHICAGO, The Art Institute of Chicago: *The White Crucifixion*, 1938: p. 26, p. 27 (details) | LIÈGE, Museum of Modern and Contemporary Art Liège: *The Blue House*, 1917-1920: cover (detail), p.5 | MADRID, Museo Thyssen-Bornemisza (Fundacio): *The Cock*, 1929 : p. 23 | MOSCOW, Tretyakov State Gallery: *Jewish Theatre, panel "Theatre"*, 1920: p. 14 ; *Jewish Theatre, panel "Dance"*, 1920: p. 14 ; *Jewish Theatre, panel "Music"*, 1920: p. 14 | NICE, National Museum Marc Chagall: *The Dance*, 1950-1952: cover (detail), © RMN-Grand Palais (musée Marc Chagall) / Gérard Blot | NEW YORK, Albright-Knox Art Gallery: *The Rural Life*, 1925: p. 3 ; Salomon R. Guggenheim Museum: *The Soldier Drinks*, 1911-1912: p. 2 (detail), p. 6, p. 7 (details) ; *The Green Violinist*, 1923-1924: p. 14, 19 ; MoMA: *I and the Village*, 1911 : cover, p. 2 (detail), p. 9 ; *The Birthday*, 1915: p. 2 (detail), p.12 (details), p. 13 |PARIS, The National Museum of Modern Art, Georges Pompidou Centre: *The Revolution*, 1937: p. 3 ; *Bella with white collar*, 1917: p. 31(detail) ; Opéra Garnier: *Chagall's Ceiling* 1963 : p. 30 |PHILADELPHIA, Philadelphia Museum of Art: *Self-portrait with Collar*, 1914 : p. 1 (detail), p. 16 |TUDELEY (UK), All Saints' Church, Choir, south wall: *Angels and Animals* (stained glass window), 1974: p. 28 ; *Trees and Angels* (stained glass window), 1974: p. 28.

Private Collection *Circus* , lithography M.491, 1967: p. 2 (detail), p.25 ; *The Cock and the Fox*, 1926: p. 22 ; *Birth*, 1911: p. 4 ; *Bella in profile*, 1916: p. 12 (detail) ; *The Hen,* 1927-28: cover (detail), p. 2(detail).

Photography: *Marc, Bella and Ida Chagall*, Petrograd, 1917, p. 12 ; *Marc Chagall,* around 1937, p. 22; *Marc Chagall painting the first stage of the Harlequins*, 1933, p. 24 ; *Chagall*, 1942 : p. 8, 31

Marc Chagall References :
Extract from the preface to *The Circus*, Paris, Editions Tériade, 1967: p. 24
Extract from *My Distant Home*, Poèmes, 1930-35, Genève, Cramer, 1975: p. 17
Extract from *My Life*, 1931, Editions Stock : p. 22

Others : Calvet-Rogniat : *The Fox and the Grapes* : p. 23

© Chagall®/SABAM, Brussels 2016

Thanks to: Meret Meyer, Vice President of the Marc Chagall Committee, Ambre Gauthier, the Marc Chagall Committee, Florence Pawlak, The Marc Chagall National Museum, Aurore t'Kint, Véronique Lux, Carole Daprey, Eric Vaes, Anne-Sophie Parzelt, Stuart Forward and everyone who has been involved in the production of this book.

The works of Kate'Art Editions are available in a variety of languages: French, English, Dutch, Spanish, German, Italian, Russian, Japanese and Danish.

Visit our online shop: **www.kateart.com**